QUICK THINKING™

Critical and Creative Thinking Challenges
Grades K-6

by
Beverly Cunningham

© 1992, 1995
ECS Learning Systems, Inc.
P.O. Box 791437
San Antonio, Texas 78279
210-438-4262

Printed in the U.S.A.

Page Layout & Graphics: Kathryn Riches

Cover/Book Design: Educational Media Services

Other Titles from the Think and Learn™ Series:

ECS0492	**Geometry**	**(Grades 2-5)**
ECS045X	**Money**	**(Grades 2-5)**
ECS000X	**Novel Extenders, Book 1**	**(Grades 1-3)**
ECS0018	**Novel Extenders, Book 2**	**(Grades 1-3)**
ECS0069	**Novel Extenders, Book 3**	**(Grades 1-3)**
ECS0077	**Novel Extenders, Book 4**	**(Grades 1-3)**
ECS9072	**Writing Warm-Ups™**	**(Grades K-6)**
ECS9455	**Writing Warm-Ups™ Two**	**(Grades K-6)**

To order, contact your local school supply store, or write/call:

ECS Learning Systems, Inc.
P.O. Box 791437
San Antonio, Texas 78279–1437
1-800-68-TEACH

ISBN 0-944459-47-1

TABLE OF CONTENTS

Introduction   4

Using Quick Thinking   5

Seven Ways of Learning   6

General Challenges   7

Science Challenges   21

Social Studies Challenges   35

Mathematics Challenges   49

Language Arts Challenges   63

References   77

INTRODUCTION

Quick Thinking Challenges are critical and creative thinking activities for teachers who want students to make the most of every minute in the classroom. Organized into five subject areas, each thinking challenge is presented in a simple, easy-to-use format. The extensions included with each challenge are organized into seven different ways of learning. They challenge students to think critically and creatively on a variety of topics in different subject areas.

HOW?

Quick Thinking Challenges belong in every classroom. Challenges can be as brief or as extended as you choose. The extensions allow the student to explore a topic in a variety of learning ways. You have many options for using Quick Thinking Challenges in your classroom.

WHO?

Critical and creative thinking skills are important for everyone. Primary students might choose challenges which generate oral language. Intermediate students might choose challenges which involve oral and written activities. The student may choose from a variety of extensions that emphasize different learning styles.

WHEN?

Quick Thinking Challenges can spark a class at the beginning, middle, or end of a day. Use them to challenge your students while you take roll or manage other paper work. Use them as a sponge activity for the minutes at the end of class when you finish early and do not want to begin a new topic. Use them to extend the students' learning outside the classroom. Use challenges to extend your students' critical and creative thinking.

WHY?

Seven different kinds of intelligence are described in Howard Gardner's *Frames of Mind:*

> verbal/linguistic
> logical/mathematical
> visual/spatial
> body/kinesthetic
> musical/rhythmic
> interpersonal
> intrapersonal

Gardner's model gives the teacher a way of looking at the complete picture of the learner's potential. Most classrooms teach to the verbal/ linguistic and logical/mathematical intelligences. All seven intelligences are included in the extension section of each challenge.

USING QUICK THINKING

The following section explains how the challenges appear and offers suggestions for using them in your classroom. Each challenge is divided into three sections. The first section includes an open-ended question or statement. The second section lists critical and creative thinking skills as they relate to the challenge. The last section includes three or more extensions which address the different ways students learn. Read over this information before you begin using the challenges with your students.

Challenge:

Each activity begins with an open-ended question or statement.

Thinking Skills:

All challenges require critical and creative thinking. This section lists some of the critical and creative thinking skills that students will probably use in response to the challenge.

There are many **critical thinking skills**. Quick Thinking Challenges incorporate one or more of three critical thinking skills.

Analysis is the ability to take an idea apart and examine its parts or sections. It requires the skills of observing, identifying critical attributes, classifying, or comparing.

Synthesis is the ability to put ideas together in a different or unique way. It requires the skills of designing, rearranging, or changing.

Evaluation is the ability to make judgments or rate the value of something. It requires judging, measuring, or deciding.

Creative thinking skills are also part of each challenge. Quick Thinking Challenges incorporate one or more of eight creative thinking skills.

Fluency is the ability to produce a large quantity of ideas, answers, or solutions.

Flexibility is the ability to produce many different kinds of ideas, answers, or solutions.

Originality is the ability to produce unique and unusual ideas, answers, or solutions.

Elaboration is the ability to provide new and meaningful details to ideas, answers, or solutions.

Risk-taking is the ability to take a chance, to experiment, or to try different ideas, answers, or solutions.

Complexity is the ability to deal with intricate ideas and bring order through answers or solutions.

Curiosity is the ability to wonder or question puzzling ideas, answers, or solutions.

Imagination is the ability to visualize beyond the limits of ideas, answers, or solutions.

Extensions:

Students are individuals with distinct personal learning styles. Howard Gardner's theory of multiple intelligences provides a foundation upon which to identify and develop the students' multiple abilities.

Each challenge is extended with an activity in three or more of the seven kinds of intelligences. Space is provided for the teacher to make notes or extensions of his/her own. Use this space to extend the students' learning into all seven areas of intelligence.

SEVEN WAYS OF LEARNING

The time has come for teachers to start focusing their attention on the inner capability of each and every student. Howard Gardner's theory of multiple intelligences provides a solid foundation upon which to identify and develop a broad spectrum of abilities within each child. Everyone has all seven intelligences in different proportions. Below is a brief summary of Gardner's seven intelligences.

 Verbal/Linguistic Intelligence
These students learn best by verbalizing or hearing and seeing words.

 Logical/Mathematical Intelligence
These students explore patterns, categories, and relationships by actively manipulating things in a controlled and orderly way.

 Visual/Spatial Intelligence
These students think in images and pictures. They spend free time drawing, designing things, or simply daydreaming.

 Bodily/Kinesthetic Intelligence
These students communicate very effectively through gestures and other forms of body language. They need opportunities to learn by moving or acting things out.

 Musical/Rhythmic Intelligence
These students respond to music (both instrumental and environmental) and to tonal patterns and rhythms.

 Interpersonal Intelligence
These students understand people. They organize, communicate, and mediate.

 Intrapersonal Intelligence
These students have a deep awareness of their inner feelings, dreams, and ideas.

Metacognition is the process of *"thinking about thinking."* Students should learn how to question themselves about their own knowledge, thinking, and problem solving. Metacognition questions cause the student to—

* develop their own thought processes
* use specific thinking processes to problem solve
* develop new thinkng processes to address problems in alternate ways
* evaluate the effectiveness of their thinking processes
* build independent thinking skills that they carry into their adult life

Students who learn how to use and answer effective metacognitive questions will benefit in the learning process. When teachers allow students to "think about their thinking" and include metacognitive questions in their teaching, they validate these students' thinking processes. As a result, the students feel encouraged to develop and share their thinking with others.

Each of us has all of these intelligences, but not all of them are developed equally. All seven intelligences are included under each extension. This book addresses at least three different intelligences in the extension section of each challenge. When we focus on an intelligence, the gear next to that intelligence is filled in, and an activity that extends the challenge follows that gear.

Example: Focused 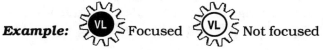Not focused

The following Quick Thinking Challenges offer practical alternatives for discovering your students' learning potential and encouraging your students' desire to learn—with all seven kinds of intelligence.

© 1992 by ECS Learning Systems, Inc., San Antonio, TX

GENERAL CHALLENGES

General Challenges

Page Numbers

Intelligence	9	10	11	12	13	14	15	16	17	18	19	20
1. Verbal/Linguistic		⚙		⚙		⚙	⚙	⚙	⚙	⚙	⚙	⚙
2. Logical/Mathematical	⚙		⚙		⚙			⚙	⚙			⚙
3. Visual/Spatial	⚙	⚙	⚙	⚙	⚙	⚙		⚙		⚙	⚙	
4. Body/Kinesthetic		⚙				⚙	⚙		⚙	⚙	⚙	
5. Musical/Rhythmic	⚙			⚙			⚙		⚙			⚙
6. Interpersonal			⚙		⚙						⚙	
7. Intrapersonal	⚙	⚙		⚙		⚙	⚙	⚙		⚙		⚙

CHALLENGE

Big is to huge as _____ is to _____.

THINKING SKILLS

CRITICAL
Analysis, compare/contrast

CREATIVE
Flexibility, elaboration

EXTENSIONS

(VL)

(LM) *Pattern games*—Use pattern blocks to model the pattern expressed in the challenge. How many more examples can you show with pattern blocks?

(VS) *Patterns/Designs*—Draw a pattern that reinforces the challenge, or cut pictures from a magazine and arrange them in a pattern to demonstrate the challenge.

(BK)

(MR) *Tonal patterns*—Using a recorder or other musical instrument, how many different tonal patterns can you play that are expressed by the challenge?

(INT)

(INR) *Metacognition question*—How could I state this problem/situation in a different way?

CHALLENGE

List five new ways to go to school.

THINKING SKILLS

CRITICAL	CREATIVE
Analysis	Fluency, flexibility, originality

EXTENSIONS

 Directions—Explain how to find your classroom from the library, the cafeteria, and the bus area.

_____

_____

 Mind-mapping—Learn how to use "mind-mapping" as a note-taking process.

_____

 Role playing—Select a community helper and demonstrate his/her assistance in your safe arrival at school.

_____

_____

_____

 Metacognition questions—What other information will I need to solve this problem? How could I use this information in my everyday life?

10

CHALLENGE

Make a list of things that are small and red.

THINKING SKILLS

CRITICAL
Analysis

CREATIVE
Fluency, imagination

EXTENSIONS

Problem solving—Write a story problem using "small red items" from your list.

Drawing—Draw a picture using only a red crayon or marker. How does it make you feel? Would a different color have a different effect on you?

Communication—Some students wear small, red ribbons to "say NO to drugs." Discuss "Saying NO to Drugs." What new strategies can you recommend? Share these strategies with a friend.

CHALLENGE

You have a paper clip, a tissue, and some string. What could you make?

THINKING SKILLS

CRITICAL	CREATIVE
Analysis, synthesis	Flexibility, originality, curiosity, imagination

EXTENSIONS

 Creative writing—Write about your new "invention." Include information about its applications.

_____

_____

 Drawing—Draw a picture of your new invention.

_____

_____

 Instrumental sounds—Create a musical instrument. What sounds can you create?

_____

_____

 Metacognition questions—How many different ways could I solve this problem/situation? Does my strategy for solving this problem/situation seem to be working?

CHALLENGE

Look at the people in your classroom. How could you sort them into three groups?

THINKING SKILLS

CRITICAL
Analysis, classification

CREATIVE
Flexibility, complexity

EXTENSIONS

(VL)

_____

(LM) *Graphic organizers*—Classify your classmates into a "people graph" by moving them into columns by clothes, shoes, color of hair, etc. Chart your results.

_____

(VS) *Patterns/Designs*—Classify your classmates by the geometric designs you see in their clothing. Organize them into groups and have students question—why?

_____

(BK)

_____

(MR)

_____

(INT) *Group activity*—Use a "human graph" to see where a group stands on an issue or idea.

_____

(INR)

CHALLENGE

Outside is to inside as _____ is to _____ .

THINKING SKILLS

CRITICAL
Analysis, compare/contrast

CREATIVE
Flexibility, elaboration

EXTENSIONS

VL *Vocabulary*—Use a thesaurus and compile a list of as many contrasting words as possible in a given time limit. Share your list in a brainstorming activity.

LM

VS *Drawing*—Draw pictures of things the way they would look under a microscope.

BK *Games*—Adapt an outside game as an inside activity for your classmates. What changes will you have to make?

MR

INT

INR *Metacognition questions*—Does this problem seem easy or difficult to solve? Why?

CHALLENGE

Create a class flag. Explain what it means.

THINKING SKILLS

CRITICAL
Analysis, synthesis

CREATIVE
Flexibility, originality

EXTENSIONS

 Storytelling—Tell a story about the country your flag flies over (real or imaginary).

 Folk/Creative dance—Create a national dance to accompany your new flag. Bring out the meaning of the flag in your dance.

 Musical composition—Create a national song to accompany your new flag. Bring out the meaning of the flag in your song.

 Metacognition question—What will be my first step in solving the challenge? This challenge is enjoyable/not enjoyable because...

CHALLENGE

List five ways you could improve your school desk.

THINKING SKILLS

CRITICAL	CREATIVE
Analysis	Fluency, flexibility, originality

EXTENSIONS

Poetry—Write a poem describing the good points of your improved school desk.
Advertising—Write an ad or present a commercial to sell your improved school desk.

_____

Problem solving—Design a desk for schools of the future. What will you include? What will you omit?

_____

Advertising—Record the ad/commercial to sell your improved school desk on video tape. Present it to the class. What did you do visually to "sell" your product?

_____

_____

_____

_____

Metacognition questions—How many different ways could I solve this challenge? Does my strategy for solving this challenge seem to be working?

_____

CHALLENGE

Imagine that you had to keep a baby happy for one hour. What would you do?

THINKING SKILLS

CRITICAL
Analysis, synthesis

CREATIVE
Flexibility, originality, imagination

EXTENSIONS

 Reading—Select a variety of interesting storybooks with bright, colorful pictures. Read them aloud, with expression.

 Problem solving—Set a timer for fifteen minutes. Do a game or activity which will fill this time. Repeat with a different game or activity three more times. By breaking the hour into four parts, does your time pass faster?

 Mime—Pretend you are a clown. Pantomime your clown act from the circus.

 Humming/Singing—Hum or sing a variety of nursery rhymes or children's songs in a cheerful voice.

CHALLENGE

How many different ways can you say good-bye?

THINKING SKILLS

CRITICAL
Analysis, synthesis

CREATIVE
Fluency, flexibility, originality

EXTENSIONS

 Vocabulary—List the different ways to say good-bye in as many different foreign languages as you can find. Try to find someone who speaks another language and record their "good-bye."

 Pictures—Gather as many different pictures as you can that show someone saying "good-bye."

 Mime—Pantomime different ways to say "good-bye" with your face and your body.

 Metacognition questions—What new words do I find in this challenge? How do the pictures and illustrations go with this challenge?

 © 1992 by ECS Learning Systems, Inc., San Antonio, TX

CHALLENGE

List the good and bad points of television.

THINKING SKILLS

CRITICAL
Analysis, compare/contrast

CREATIVE
Fluency, elaboration

EXTENSIONS

 Journal/Diary keeping—Establish criteria for judging television shows. Keep a journal and rank television shows according to your criteria. Create your own rating system.

_____

_____

 Advertising—Design an ad for your favorite/least favorite T.V. program. Appeal to the audience using pictures and color.

_____

 Mime—Pretend to be a character from your favorite T.V. show.

_____

 Group activity—Present a debate which focuses on the good/bad points of television. Each group must defend a side, either good or bad, with at least three points.

_____

_____

CHALLENGE

You have a marble, a pencil, and a cup. What could you make?

THINKING SKILLS

CRITICAL	**CREATIVE**
Analysis, synthesis	Flexibility, originality, curiosity, imagination

EXTENSIONS

 Impromptu speaking—Describe your new "invention," including its applications. Use a basic format for the presentation decided on by the class.

 Problem solving—Invent a new game using the items provided in the challenge. Give directions for your new game. Provide an opportunity for your classmates to play the game.

 Rhythmic patterns—Create a rhythm using only the items provided in the challenge. Can you create a rhythmic pattern?

 Metacognition questions—How many different ways could I solve this challenge? What will be my first step in solving this challenge?

SCIENCE CHALLENGES

Science Challenges

Intelligence	Page Numbers											
	23	24	25	26	27	28	29	30	31	32	33	34
1. Verbal/Linguistic	⚙	⚙		⚙	⚙	⚙	⚙	⚙	⚙		⚙	⚙
2. Logical/Mathematical		⚙	⚙	⚙			⚙	⚙	⚙			
3. Visual/Spatial	⚙	⚙	⚙		⚙	⚙		⚙		⚙	⚙	⚙
4. Body/Kinesthetic			⚙	⚙	⚙	⚙	⚙		⚙	⚙		⚙
5. Musical/Rhythmic		⚙				⚙			⚙		⚙	
6. Interpersonal	⚙			⚙				⚙		⚙		
7. Intrapersonal			⚙		⚙	⚙	⚙				⚙	⚙

CHALLENGE

Cloud is to rain as _____ is to _____.

THINKING SKILLS

CRITICAL
Analysis, compare/contrast

CREATIVE
Flexibility, originality, elaboration

EXTENSIONS

VL *Creative writing*—Write and illustrate weather poems or personification stories about clouds, rain, hail, tornadoes, or some other type of weather. Add sound effects when presenting your selection to classmates.

LM

VS *Imagination*—Lie on the grass and look up at the sky. What shapes do you see in the sky? Describe the shapes you see in the sky to your classmates.

BK

MR

INT *Group activity*—Each group researches environmental effects of water conservation. Prepare a consumer's guide for fifty ways to conserve water.

INR

CHALLENGE

The answer is "whales and dolphins." What is the question?

THINKING SKILLS

CRITICAL
Analysis, compare/contrast

CREATIVE
Fluency, flexibility, originality

EXTENSIONS

 Writing—Write an index or table of contents for a book on whales and dolphins. What topics would you be sure to include?

 Graphic organizers—Use graph paper and make a scale drawing of a whale and/or a dolphin. As a group activity, transfer the whale drawing to a grid marked on the playground or parking lot.

 Pictures—Create a collage on whales and dolphins. Use pictures from magazines, or draw your own.

 Environmental sounds—Whales use echolocation, a high-pitch sound, to locate objects. Working with a blindfolded partner, communicate like whales by sending out signals. After you have located your partner, change places in the activity.

24   © 1992 by ECS Learning Systems, Inc., San Antonio, TX   All rights reserved

CHALLENGE

Muscles are like _____ because...

THINKING SKILLS

CRITICAL
Analysis, synthesis, evaluation

CREATIVE
Flexibility, originality, elaboration, curiosity

EXTENSIONS

(VL)

_____

(LM) *Graphic organizers*—Create a web that shows the attributes of the muscular system.

_____

(VS) *Pretending*—Pretend you are a simple machine. What muscles do you use to operate? Visualize your machine on and off.

_____

(BK) *Physical exercise*—Perform physical exercise routines to music. Notice which muscles you are using.

_____

(MR)

_____

(INT)

_____

(INR) *Metacognition questions*—What other information will I need to understand this challenge? How could I use this information in my everyday life?

CHALLENGE

How many mammals that live in the woods can you list?

THINKING SKILLS

CRITICAL
Analysis

CREATIVE
Fluency, flexibility

EXTENSIONS

 Creative writing—"Become" a mammal. Write about a day in the woods from your point of view.

 Problem solving—Begin with four deer hunting for food. What would be the effects of drought, flooding, hunters, etc. on your life as a deer?

 Mime—Play charades. Take turns being different mammals. What actions can you use?

 Communication—Each group "becomes" a different mammal. Study your mammal and share your ways to communicate. Make a communication cube. On each face of the cube, discuss a different way your mammal communicates. Use words and pictures.

CHALLENGE

List all the ways you could use magnets in your home.

THINKING SKILLS

CRITICAL	CREATIVE
Analysis	Fluency, flexibility, elaboration

EXTENSIONS

 Creative writing—You are a car, but your back bumper is a magnet. What kinds of problems do you encounter on your drive to work?

_____

_____

 Pretending—Pretend you are a magnetized garbage separator/collector. Draw what you would look like.

_____

 Role playing—Select some students to be different types of magnets and some students to be items around your home. Which items will be attracted to the magnets? Why? Role play the magnetic attraction.

_____

_____

_____

 Metacognition question—How could I use this information in my everyday life?

_____

CHALLENGE

Wind is helpful when...

THINKING SKILLS

CRITICAL
Analysis, synthesis

CREATIVE
Fluency, elaboration

EXTENSIONS

 Writing—Write questions for interviewing a meteorologist. What would you like to know about weather?

_____

_____

 Sculpture—Make a sailboat. Does the size of the sail affect your boat? How?

_____

 Body language—On a windy day, go outside and stand first facing the wind, then with your back to the wind. Describe the sensations to a friend.

_____

 Instrumental sounds—When the wind is blowing, what environmental sounds do you hear? What musical instruments are played by blowing? Can you make an instrument that you blow through?

_____

_____

 Metacognition questions—What do I already know about this subject? What would I like to know about this subject?

28 © 1992 by ECS Learning Systems, Inc., San Antonio, TX

CHALLENGE

The answer is "volcanoes and earthquakes." What is the question?

THINKING SKILLS

CRITICAL
Analysis, compare/contrast

CREATIVE
Fluency, flexibility, originality

EXTENSIONS

 Storytelling—Write story parts about a volcano or an earthquake on an old shower curtain. Place it on the floor and hop a story.

 Graphic organizers—Make a chart about volcanoes and/or earthquakes. What we know, what we want to know, and what we learned are the three columns in the chart. As a class, complete the first two columns. After you study, complete the last column.

 Role playing—Be a piece of volcanic lava spewing out and flowing down the side of a volcano. Share your journey with your classmates.

 Metacognition question—How could I illustrate/diagram what I have learned from this material/experience?

CHALLENGE

How would the ground look to you if you were an ant?

THINKING SKILLS

CRITICAL	CREATIVE
Analysis	Originality, curiosity, imagination

EXTENSIONS

 Storytelling—Tell a story from an ant's point of view.

_____

 Problem solving—Create a solution for an ant with too much food to carry home. How does he get help?

_____

 Drawing—Draw five different items found outside on the ground from an ant's point of view.

_____

_____

_____

 Communication—You have discovered a picnic near your ant hill. How will you "speak" to your fellow ants about this food supply you have discovered?

_____

CHALLENGE

Dinosaurs are like _____ because...

THINKING SKILLS

CRITICAL
Analysis, synthesis

CREATIVE
Flexibility, originality, elaboration

EXTENSIONS

VL *Jokes/Humor*—Write dinosaur jokes using information gathered from the library.

LM *Pattern games*—Use pictures of dinosaurs and their footprints. Create a concentration memory game that asks players to match dinosaurs with the correct footprints. Other possible match-ups are dinosaur/fact or dinosaur/dinosaur.

VS

BK *Drama*—Create a dinosaur drama. Present the drama for the class.

MR *Singing*—Set dinosaur facts to music. Teach the songs to the class.

INT

INR

CHALLENGE

What are all the ways that you know when it is spring?

THINKING SKILLS

CRITICAL	CREATIVE
Analysis	Fluency, flexibility, originality

EXTENSIONS

Drawing—Invent a new spring holiday. Write it on the calendar, and then make a banner, poster, or song describing it.

Physical gestures—Select several wind poems from the library. Share these poems using physical gestures. Involve your classmates with pinwheels or wind chimes for emphasis.

Group activity—Read spring poetry from different perspectives. You might be a flower, a green meadow, or an animal in the meadow. How will your point of view affect your reading?

CHALLENGE

Design a machine that would help plants grow better. Explain how it works.

THINKING SKILLS

CRITICAL	CREATIVE
Analysis, synthesis	Flexibility, originality, curiosity, imagination

EXTENSIONS

 Vocabulary—Make a classroom dictionary of plants.

 Drawing—Select four or five plants from the classroom dictionary. Draw, label, and write distinguishing characteristics for each plant.

 Instrumental sounds—Write a poem that tells how sunshine sounds. Find a musical instrument that makes that sound. Have a friend accompany your poem when you share it with the class.

 Metacognition question—How do pictures and illustrations enhance this challenge?

CHALLENGE

Sun is to Earth as _____ is to _____.

THINKING SKILLS

CRITICAL
Analysis, compare/contrast

CREATIVE
Flexibility, elaboration

EXTENSIONS

VL *Imagination*—When you are studying the universe, write space fantasies. Illustrate your space fantasies through drawings or sculpture.

LM

VS *Pretending*—Build a rocket ship for space exploration. Use a large refrigerator box and decorate it. Use your imagination.

BK *Drama*—Each student represents a different planet in the solar system. Be sure to include student(s) to represent the moon(s) around each planet. Create the orbits of the planets around the sun using the students.

MR

INT

INR *Metacognition questions*—Does this problem/situation seem easy or difficult to solve? Why?

SOCIAL
STUDIES
CHALLENGES

Social Studies Challenges

Page Numbers

Intelligence	37	38	39	40	41	42	43	44	45	46	47	48
1. Verbal/ Linguistic	⚙	⚙	⚙		⚙	⚙	⚙	⚙	⚙	⚙	⚙	⚙
2. Logical/ Mathematical			⚙	⚙			⚙		⚙	⚙		⚙
3. Visual/ Spatial	⚙	⚙	⚙	⚙	⚙	⚙	⚙	⚙	⚙	⚙	⚙	
4. Body/ Kinesthetic	⚙	⚙				⚙	⚙			⚙		⚙
5. Musical/ Rhythmic		⚙			⚙			⚙			⚙	
6. Interpersonal				⚙	⚙				⚙			⚙
7. Intrapersonal	⚙		⚙			⚙	⚙	⚙			⚙	⚙

CHALLENGE

A new student in your class cannot speak English.
How could you teach him/her the way to the cafeteria?

THINKING SKILLS

CRITICAL	CREATIVE
Analysis	Flexibility, originality

EXTENSIONS

 Vocabulary—Learn basic conversational terms from a foreign language dictionary. Use this knowledge to give directions.

_____

_____

 Drawing—Draw a map to the school cafeteria including noticeable landmarks. Mark the directions with a colored marker.

_____

 Physical gestures—Create gestures to represent the directions or legend on a map.

_____

_____

_____

 Metacognition questions—What other information will I need to solve this challenge? What new words do I need for this challenge?

CHALLENGE

If I lived in another country, I would...

THINKING SKILLS

CRITICAL
Analysis, evaluation

CREATIVE
Flexibility, originality, elaboration, imagination

EXTENSIONS

 Reading—Read stories, myths, and poetry from that country.

_____

_____

 Sculpture—Make a clay map of the country. Show its geographical features. Make a legend to explain your map.

_____

 Folk/Creative dance—Learn a folk dance from your country. Teach it to the class.

_____

 Singing—Learn a folk song from your country. Teach it to the class.

_____

_____

CHALLENGE

Rules are to school as _____ is to _____.

THINKING SKILLS

CRITICAL
Analysis, compare/contrast

CREATIVE
Flexibility, elaboration

EXTENSIONS

VL — *Vocabulary*—Create a word collage on important people in your school, community, state, nation, or world today.

LM — *Outlining*—Compare and contrast different people or periods of history. Have a list of information to gather on each one.

VS — *Pictures*—Organize a photo essay on important people in your school, community, state, nation, or world today.

BK

MR

INT

INR — *Metacognition questions*—I would still like to know...How could I summarize what I have learned?

CHALLENGE

List three ways that three students could improve
the school playground in three minutes.

THINKING SKILLS

CRITICAL
Analysis

CREATIVE
Flexibility, originality

EXTENSIONS

Sequences—Create a jump rope rhyme that sequences the school playground equipment in a given order. Would it be more fun if they were sequenced in a different order?

Drawing—Create and illustrate an advertisement for school playground equipment. How will this new equipment improve your school playground?

Person-to-person—Teach a jump rope rhyme to a classmate.

CHALLENGE

Make a list of hot places to live.

THINKING SKILLS

CRITICAL	CREATIVE
Analysis	Fluency, flexibility, originality

EXTENSIONS

 Vocabulary—Write a travel brochure for any hot place to live.

_____

_____

 Pictures—Illustrate a travel brochure for any hot place to live. Use pictures cut from magazines or drawings you have done.

_____

_____

 Instrumental sounds—Listen to different music selections. Analyze different climates through their music. Does the location of a country affect its music?

_____

 Group activity—Pretend you are on a desert island. Brainstorm what you might need to survive. Each group lists the five items they would need for survival. Give reasons for your choices.

_____

CHALLENGE

What are all the different ways you can show you love your country?

THINKING SKILLS

CRITICAL
Analysis, synthesis

CREATIVE
Fluency, flexibility, elaboration

EXTENSIONS

 Scrapbook—Make a scrapbook of newspaper and magazine articles or pictures that show you love your country.

_____

_____

 Painting—Paint a mural that shows you love your country. What symbols would you include?

_____

 Role playing—Role play a conversation with an important historical figure. How did this person show pride in his/her country?

_____

_____

_____

 Metacognition questions—What do I already know about this subject? What will be my first step in solving this problem/situation?

  © 1992 by ECS Learning Systems, Inc., San Antonio, TX

CHALLENGE

A good citizen always _____ because...

THINKING SKILLS

CRITICAL	CREATIVE
Analysis, synthesis	Fluency, flexibility, originality, elaboration

EXTENSIONS

(VL) *Speech*—Write a speech that a good citizen would give to his/her community. Give the speech to your classmates.

(LM) *Sequencing*—Sequence the criteria for being a good citizen from most important to least important.

(VS) *Award*—Create an award a good citizen would receive.

(BK) *Body language*—Organize a patriotic parade. Who would march in the parade? What would they do to show their patriotism?

(MR)

(INT)

(INR) *Metacognition questions*—How should I organize my answer/response? How could I use this information in my everyday life?

CHALLENGE

Imagine there was a contest called "Make a Pretty City."
What would you do to make a prettier city?

THINKING SKILLS

CRITICAL
Analysis, synthesis

CREATIVE
Originality, elaboration, imagination

EXTENSIONS

 Poetry or Journal—Write a descriptive poem about a city, or keep a journal on the "Beautification of Your City."

_____

_____

 Painting—Illustrate your poem or journal entry with a skyline painting.
Drawing—Draw a bumper sticker that encourages a "Pretty City."

_____

_____

 Song/Jingle—Write a song or jingle about how you would make a prettier city. Teach it to your classmates.

_____

_____

 Metacognition questions—How would pictures and illustrations go with this challenge? How could I use this information in my city?

CHALLENGE

Person is to town as _____ is to _____.

THINKING SKILLS

CRITICAL
Analysis, compare/contrast

CREATIVE
Flexibility, elaboration

EXTENSIONS

VL *Directions*—Study a road map of your town. Give verbal instructions to a friend to travel from one location to another location.

LM *Deciphering codes*—Study the legend on a map. Teach someone else the legend's key.

VS *Drawing*—Create your own legend for a map you draw of your "make-believe" town. Color code your map.

BK

MR

INT *Communication*—Learn to read different kinds of maps, and then teach another student how to understand them.

INR

CHALLENGE

You are a sailor on the *Santa Maria*. What frightens you?

THINKING SKILLS

CRITICAL
Analysis

CREATIVE
Fluency, elaboration, curiosity

EXTENSIONS

 Storytelling—Tell a story about your favorite experience as a sailor.

 Sequencing—Create a time line to sequence the events leading to the discovery of America.

 Watercolor—Illustrate your story about your experience as a sailor with pictures, drawings, or paintings. Be sure to include special events.

 Drama—You have just discovered America in 1492. Dramatize your experiences as a sailor arriving on one of Christopher Columbus' ships.

© 1992 by ECS Learning Systems, Inc., San Antonio, TX

CHALLENGE

Towns are like _____ because...

THINKING SKILLS

CRITICAL
Analysis, compare/contrast, synthesis

CREATIVE
Fluency, flexibility, originality, elaboration

EXTENSIONS

VL *Newspaper*—Write a headline for a special event in your town today.

_____

LM

_____

VS *Drawing*—Imagine what you think your town will be like in ten years. Draw what you see.

_____

BK

_____

MR *Environmental sounds*—Select a favorite location in your town. What sounds do you hear in the morning and at night?

_____

INT

_____

INR *Metacognition questions*—Does this problem/situation seem easy or difficult to solve? Why? How many different ways could I solve this problem/situation?

CHALLENGE

What could you see in a city that you couldn't see in the country?

THINKING SKILLS

CRITICAL
Analysis, compare/contrast, synthesis

CREATIVE
Fluency, flexibility, originality, elaboration

EXTENSIONS

 Reading—Read *The City Mouse and the Country Mouse.* Compare and contrast their life styles.

 Problem solving—Select a problem the country mouse had, and solve it from the city mouse's point of view. Select a problem the city mouse had, and solve it from the country mouse's point of view. Explain the different ways of looking at the same problem.

 Role playing—First role play the city mouse. Then role play the country mouse. How do your actions differ?

 Group activity—Owls eat mice, but what do mice eat? Divide into small groups and become "food chain detectives." Share the results of your detective work with the class.

 Metacognition question—How many different ways could I solve this challenge?

MATHEMATICS CHALLENGES

Mathematics Challenges

Page Numbers

Intelligence	51	52	53	54	55	56	57	58	59	60	61	62
1. Verbal/Linguistic	⚙			⚙	⚙		⚙	⚙	⚙	⚙	⚙	⚙
2. Logical/Mathematical		⚙	⚙			⚙	⚙			⚙	⚙	
3. Visual/Spatial	⚙		⚙	⚙	⚙	⚙		⚙	⚙	⚙		⚙
4. Body/Kinesthetic	⚙	⚙		⚙	⚙		⚙			⚙		⚙
5. Musical/Rhythmic			⚙		⚙			⚙	⚙			
6. Interpersonal	⚙					⚙			⚙		⚙	
7. Intrapersonal		⚙	⚙	⚙		⚙	⚙	⚙		⚙	⚙	⚙

CHALLENGE

Give five ways to get the answer 6.

THINKING SKILLS

CRITICAL	CREATIVE
Analysis	Flexibility, originality, elaboration

EXTENSIONS

 Creative writing—Write a play about the "Wonderful World of Six." Present your play for the class.

 Drawing—Create a picture using only the number six. Use as many sixes as you want to complete your picture. Display your picture.

 Body language—Create numbers using your body. See how many different numbers you can create using two people, three people, or four people.

 Group activity—Divide into groups with six students in each group. What activity can you do with six students that you cannot do with two, three, or four students?

CHALLENGE

▲ is to ■ as _____ is to _____ .

THINKING SKILLS

CRITICAL
Analysis, compare/contrast

CREATIVE
Flexibility, elaboration

EXTENSIONS

(VL)

_____

(LM) *Pattern games*—Use pattern blocks to create a pattern with shapes missing. You complete the series. How many different patterns can you make with three different shapes, with four different shapes, and so forth?

_____

(VS)

_____

(BK) *Drama*—Create and act out a play in which the characters are geometric shapes. "Become" a geometric shape in your mind. What kinds of patterns would you create with other shapes?

_____

(MR)

_____

(INT)

_____

(INR) *Metacognition question*—What patterns do I notice as I work on this challenge?

_____

CHALLENGE

How many three-digit numbers can you make with 4, 6, 7, and 9?

THINKING SKILLS

CRITICAL
Analysis, synthesis

CREATIVE
Fluency, originality

EXTENSIONS

Number sequences—Sequence your three-digit numbers in order from least to greatest.

Color schemes—Select a color to represent each number from 0-9. Draw a picture using just three colors. What three-digit number does your picture represent?

Rhythmic patterns—Each digit receives the number of beats equal to its value. (Example: 4 = 4 beats). "Play" your three-digit number by tapping out the value of each digit. Could you write a number song?

Metacognition question—Does my strategy for answering this question seem to be working?

CHALLENGE

List your likes and dislikes for word problems.

THINKING SKILLS

CRITICAL	**CREATIVE**
Analysis, compare/contrast	Fluency, elaboration

EXTENSIONS

 Verbal debate—Divide the class in half. Hold a debate for and against word problems. Each side must have at least three supporting reasons.

_____

_____

 Drawing—Illustrate your favorite word problem.

_____

 Drama—Dramatize an addition or subtraction word problem. Characters could hold cards to represent signs or symbols.

_____

_____

_____

 Metacognition questions—How should I organize my response? What are the most important words in word problems?

 © 1992 by ECS Learning Systems, Inc., San Antonio, TX

CHALLENGE

How many different numbers can you make with 2, 4, and 7?

THINKING SKILLS

CRITICAL	**CREATIVE**
Analysis, synthesis	Fluency, originality

EXTENSIONS

 Creative writing—Select a number you created in the challenge and write a paragraph about that number. You might write about the number's family, favorite sport, or favorite hobby.

 Pattern/Design—Create a pattern or design using the numbers 2, 4, and 7.

 Role playing—Three students hold the numbers 2, 4, and 7 on cards. Create different numbers by arranging the students in a different order.

 Rhythmic patterns—Play a song in $\frac{4}{4}$ rhythm. Clap the beats for a whole note, a half-note, and a quarter-note.

CHALLENGE

↑ is to ➜ as _____ is to _____ .

THINKING SKILLS

CRITICAL
Analysis, compare/contrast

CREATIVE
Flexibility, elaboration

EXTENSIONS

VL

LM *Directions*—Using only symbols or pictures, give directions for going from your classroom to the playground.

VS *Patterns/Designs*—Using only arrows, design a picture to display in your classroom.

BK

MR

INT *Communication*—Face your friend for one minute. Observe details. Now stand back to back and describe what (s)he is wearing.

INR *Metacognition question*—What patterns do I notice as I work on this challenge?

CHALLENGE

Write a riddle that has the answer 21.

THINKING SKILLS

CRITICAL
Analysis, synthesis

CREATIVE
Fluency, originality, curiosity

EXTENSIONS

 Humor—Publish a classroom book of math riddles.

 Problem solving—Play the "Game of 21" with a partner. Count to twenty-one beginning at one. You may count by one or two numbers at a time. The person who says "21" first wins!

 Body language—Make as many numbers as you can with your whole body.

 Metacognition questions—Does this problem/situation seem easy or difficult to solve? Why? How should I organize my answer/response?

CHALLENGE

How many two-digit numbers can you make with 8, 1, 3, and 2?

THINKING SKILLS

CRITICAL
Analysis, synthesis

CREATIVE
Fluency, originality

EXTENSIONS

 Directions—Explain how to work a problem to others while they listen.

_____

_____

 Patterns—Use a story board and manipulatives to explain a problem while your partner listens.

_____

_____

 Rhythmic patterns—Learn addition and subtraction facts through drum beats.

_____

_____

 Metacognition question—What will be my first step in solving this challenge?

_____

CHALLENGE

Numbers are like _____ because...

THINKING SKILLS

CRITICAL
Analysis, synthesis

CREATIVE
Flexibility, originality, elaboration

EXTENSIONS

(VL) *Creative writing*—Make a "no number" booklet telling what the world would be like without numbers.

_____

(LM)

_____

(VS) *Drawing*—Draw a face using only numbers. Where do you use your straight numbers? Where do you use your curved numbers?

_____

(BK)

_____

(MR) *Rhythmic patterns*—Find all the songs that include numbers or counting patterns. Sing these songs with your classmates.

_____

(INT) *Group activity*—Work in groups of 2, 3, 4, etc. What size group do you prefer? Why?

_____

(INR)

CHALLENGE

Draw a picture that shows this problem: 16 – 7 = 9

THINKING SKILLS

CRITICAL
Analysis, synthesis

CREATIVE
Originality, elaboration, imagination

EXTENSIONS

 Creative writing—Write a story problem using the problem 16 – 7 = 9. Read your problem to the class.

 Formulas—Show the inverse operation of your challenge problem (addition/subtraction).

 Drawing—Draw another picture that illustrates 16 – 7 = 9.

 Drama—Act out the problem: 16 – 7 = 9.

 Metacognition questions—How many different ways could I solve this problem? How can I use the information I have learned in a new way?

© 1992 by ECS Learning Systems, Inc., San Antonio, TX

CHALLENGE

If we didn't have numbers...

THINKING SKILLS

CRITICAL	CREATIVE
Analysis, evaluation	Flexibility, originality, elaboration

EXTENSIONS

 Creative writing—Write a story about a land without numbers.

_____

 Problem solving—How would you measure or cook without numbers? Provide a solution after brainstorming in your group.

_____

_____

_____

_____

 Group activities—Share your group's solutions to the cooking problem. How important are numbers to cooking?

_____

 Metacognition questions—How do I depend on numbers in my life? What would be the greatest change in my life if there weren't any numbers?

_____

61

CHALLENGE

How could you measure the length of a room if you didn't have
a ruler or measuring tape?

THINKING SKILLS

CRITICAL
Analysis, synthesis

CREATIVE
Flexibility, originality, risk-taking

EXTENSIONS

 Reading—Listen as your teacher reads part of *Gulliver's Travels*.

_____

_____

 Imagination—After listening to parts of *Gulliver's Travels*, pretend you are a giant looking into your classroom. Describe what you see.

_____

 Physical gestures—Use different parts of your body to measure things in your classroom. Compare your measurements.

_____

_____

_____

 Metacognition questions—How many different ways could I solve this problem? Does my strategy for solving this problem seem to be working?

LANGUAGE ARTS CHALLENGES

Page Numbers

Intelligence	65	66	67	68	69	70	71	72	73	74	75	76
1. Verbal/Linguistic	⚙		⚙	⚙			⚙	⚙	⚙	⚙		⚙
2. Logical/Mathematical		⚙			⚙	⚙			⚙			⚙
3. Visual/Spatial	⚙	⚙	⚙			⚙		⚙		⚙	⚙	
4. Body/Kinesthetic	⚙			⚙	⚙		⚙		⚙		⚙	
5. Musical/Rhythmic			⚙		⚙	⚙	⚙	⚙		⚙	⚙	⚙
6. Interpersonal		⚙				⚙		⚙				⚙
7. Intrapersonal	⚙		⚙	⚙	⚙		⚙		⚙	⚙	⚙	

CHALLENGE

Make a list of five "fuzzy" words. Write a "fuzzy" sentence.

THINKING SKILLS

CRITICAL	CREATIVE
Analysis	Fluency, flexibility, originality

EXTENSIONS

 Creative writing—Write a paragraph which begins, "Today I found a fuzzy..."

_____

_____

 Drawing—Illustrate one of your "fuzzy" words. Display your drawing in a "fuzzy" gallery.

_____

 Mime—Act out one of your "fuzzy" words. Can your classmates guess what you are?

_____

_____

_____

 Metacognition questions—Does this problem seem easy or difficult to solve? Why? How could I use this information in my everyday life?

CHALLENGE

Create a new title for your favorite book.

THINKING SKILLS

CRITICAL
Analysis, synthesis

CREATIVE
Flexibility, originality, imagination

EXTENSIONS

Sequencing—Make a time line showing the major events in your favorite book.

Drawing—Design a book cover for your favorite book. Include the title and author on the cover. You become the cover illustrator.

Group activity—Start a story. Have each member of the group add a sentence. Read your group story to the class.

CHALLENGE

How many new sentences can you make by changing the underlined word?
The dog <u>barked</u> at me.

THINKING SKILLS

CRITICAL
Analysis, synthesis

CREATIVE
Fluency, originality, elaboration

EXTENSIONS

 Vocabulary—Using a thesaurus, change the underlined word in the new sentences you have written.

_____

_____

 Drawing—Select one of your new sentences. Illustrate it.

_____

_____

 Environmental sounds—Make the sounds your new underlined words suggest. Record these sounds on a tape recorder. Play the sounds. Let the class match the sound to the sentence.

_____

_____

 Metacognition question—How do the pictures and illustrations enhance this challenge?

_____

CHALLENGE

What might have happened if Paddington had been an alligator
instead of a bear?

THINKING SKILLS

CRITICAL
Evaluation

CREATIVE
Fluency, originality, elaboration

EXTENSIONS

VL *Storytelling*—Select one of Paddington's stories, and retell it from an alligator's point of view. What do you have to change in your story?

_____

LM

_____

_____

VS

_____

BK *Role playing*—Pretend to be an alligator. How will you greet your friends? How will you carry your suitcase? Will you wear a raincoat and hat?

_____

MR

_____

_____

INT

_____

INR *Metacognition questions*—How many different ways could I solve this problem/situation? If I had to solve a similar problem/situation, I would... Does my strategy for solving this problem seem to be working?

_____

© 1992 by ECS Learning Systems, Inc., San Antonio, TX

CHALLENGE

Spelling is to words as _____ is to _____.

THINKING SKILLS

CRITICAL
Analysis, compare/contrast

CREATIVE
Flexibility, elaboration

EXTENSIONS

VL

LM *Sequencing*—Organize your spelling words by syllables (two syllables, three syllables, and four syllables).

VS

BK *Physical exercise*—Select words from your list. Say them as you jump rope.

MR *Rhythmic patterns*—Find jump rope rhymes that include your spelling words. Can you find a rhythmic pattern in the jump rope rhymes?

INT

INR *Metacognition question*—What new words do I find in this challenge?

CHALLENGE

What would happen if we did not use capital letters in our writing?

THINKING SKILLS

CRITICAL
Analysis

CREATIVE
Flexibility, originality, curiosity

EXTENSIONS

Deciphering codes—A symbol, perhaps a triangle, could be placed around each letter to be capitalized as part of the "code language." Learn to read, write, and decipher "code language."

Color schemes—Select a color to represent all capital letters. Each time a letter should be capitalized, write it in the chosen color instead.

Instrumental sounds—Select a percussion instrument. Read a short story. Each time you say a word that should be capitalized play a note.

Receiving feedback—How will writing letters to be capitalized in color improve your writing? Does it help or hinder?

CHALLENGE

Make a list of "lazy" words. Write a "lazy" sentence.

THINKING SKILLS

CRITICAL	CREATIVE
Analysis	Fluency, flexibility, originality

EXTENSIONS

 Reading—Stretch out on the rug and read a story. How does your posture affect your reading?

_____

_____

_____

 Body language—Act out the nursery rhyme "Little Boy Blue." Can you find other nursery rhymes with a lazy character?

_____

 Instrumental sounds—Draw/paint a picture as a piece of music is played. How did the music affect your choice of colors?

_____

_____

 Metacognition questions—How many different ways could I solve this problem? How would I illustrate this challenge?

_____

CHALLENGE

Would you rather be a consonant or a vowel? Why?

THINKING SKILLS

CRITICAL
Analysis, evaluation

CREATIVE
Flexibility, originality, curiosity

EXTENSIONS

 Verbal debate—Hold a debate between a consonant and a vowel. Each person must defend his/her side with at least three reasons.

 Pictures—Play the vocabulary game "Pictionary."

 Instrumental sounds—Practice your weekly spelling words. When you come to a vowel, instead of saying it, tap the table.

 Communication—Brainstorm all the different ways to communicate. Record your answers to share with the class.

© 1992 by ECS Learning Systems, Inc., San Antonio, TX

CHALLENGE

What are the most important parts of a sentence? Why?

THINKING SKILLS

CRITICAL
Analysis, evaluation

CREATIVE
Fluency, elaboration, curiosity

EXTENSIONS

 Reading—Listen as your teacher reads a paragraph and leaves out the verbs. Try to guess the action words.

 Patterning—Take a paragraph, and replace all nouns with a ■ and all verbs with a ▲.

 Physical gestures—When reading your paragraph, act out the verbs instead of reading them.

 Metacognition question—How could I use this information in my everyday life?

CHALLENGE

How would the wolf explain what happened to Little Red Riding Hood?

THINKING SKILLS

CRITICAL
Analysis

CREATIVE
Fluency, originality, elaboration

EXTENSIONS

 Storytelling—Retell a favorite story from a different character's point of view.
Example: *The Three Little Pigs* retold by A. Bad Wolf.

 Imagination—Imagine being the wolf in *Little Red Riding Hood*. What would you do?

 Instrumental sounds—Play the recording *Peter and the Wolf.* Listen for the sounds that represent each character. Identify the sound the wolf makes.

 Metacognition question—How many different ways could I explain this challenge?

© 1992 by ECS Learning Systems, Inc., San Antonio, TX

CHALLENGE

Which fairy tale character is most like you? Why?

THINKING SKILLS

CRITICAL
Analysis, compare/contrast

CREATIVE
Originality, elaboration, curiosity, imagination

EXTENSIONS

Drawing—Create a cartoon or comic strip about your favorite fairy tale character. Share it with the class.

Physical exercise—Jump rope to your favorite nursery rhymes.

Instrumental sounds—Discover some sounds that will enhance the reading of your favorite fairy tale. Play the sounds while you read your favorite fairy tale.

Metacognition question—How can I use the information I have learned in a new way?

―――――― **CHALLENGE** ――――――

You have to give up two letters of the alphabet. Which ones will
you give up? Why?

―――――― **THINKING SKILLS** ――――――

CRITICAL
Analysis

CREATIVE
Flexibility, originality, curiosity

―――――― **EXTENSIONS** ――――――

 Creative writing—Write an epitaph for the two letters of the alphabet you are going to "bury."

 Problem solving—What if the two letters of the alphabet that you had to give up were **a** and **e**. How many words can you find that don't have these two letters?

 Humming—Spell a word, but hum the two letters of the alphabet you have given up. How does this affect your spelling?

 Giving feedback—How would you feel if someone else selected the letters for you to give up? Explain.

REFERENCES

Amabile, Teresa M. *Growing Up Creative*. Buffalo, New York: The Creative Education Foundation, 1989.

＊ This book has hands-on exercises and techniques that can help a parent or teacher keep creativity alive at home and at school.

Armstrong, Thomas. *In Their Own Way*. Los Angeles: Jeremy P. Tarcher, Inc., 1987.

＊ This book suggests basic improvements in the way that we help each child learn. An extensive resource section includes materials in Gardner's seven intelligences.

Caine, Renate N. and Geoffrey. *Making Connections: Teaching and the Human Brain*. Alexandria, Virginia: Association for Supervision and Curriculum Development, 1991.

＊ This book discusses the functioning of the brain under different conditions and the way learning is affected by health, stress, and teaching approaches.

Gardner, Howard. *Frames of Mind: The Theory of Multiple Intelligences*. New York: Basic Books, 1985.

＊ Gardner discusses multiple intelligences. His model of seven different kinds of intelligence gives the teacher a way of looking at the complete picture of a learner's potential.

Gardner, Howard. *The Unschooled Mind: How Children Think and How Schools Should Teach*. New York: Basic Books, 1991.

＊ Gardner makes an eloquent case for restructuring our schools, using the latest research on learning as our guide.

 **NOTES** _____